CENTRAL ASIAN IKATS

FROM THE RAU COLLECTION

CENTRAL ASIAN IKATS

FROM THE RAU COLLECTION

RUBY CLARK

V&A Publications

First published by V&A Publications, 2007
V&A Publications
Victoria and Albert Museum
South Kensington
London SW7 2RL

Distributed in North America by Harry N. Abrams, Inc., New York

Paperback edition
ISBN-13 978 1 85177 525 5
Library of Congress Control Number 2007924508

10 9 8 7 6 5 4 3 2 1
2011 2010 2009 2008 2007

A catalogue record for this book is available from the British Library.

Designed by Price Watkins
New V&A photography by Pip Barnard, V&A Photographic Studio

Front cover illustration: woman's coat (page 38)
Back cover illustration: wall hanging (page 67)
Frontispiece: wall hanging (page 61)

Printed and bound by Printing Express, Hong Kong

All illustrated ikats are from the Rau collection and were made in nineteenth-century Central Asia, unless stated otherwise. All other images are from the private archive of Pip Rau, unless stated otherwise.

V&A Publications
Victoria and Albert Museum
South Kensington
London SW7 2RL
www.vam.ac.uk

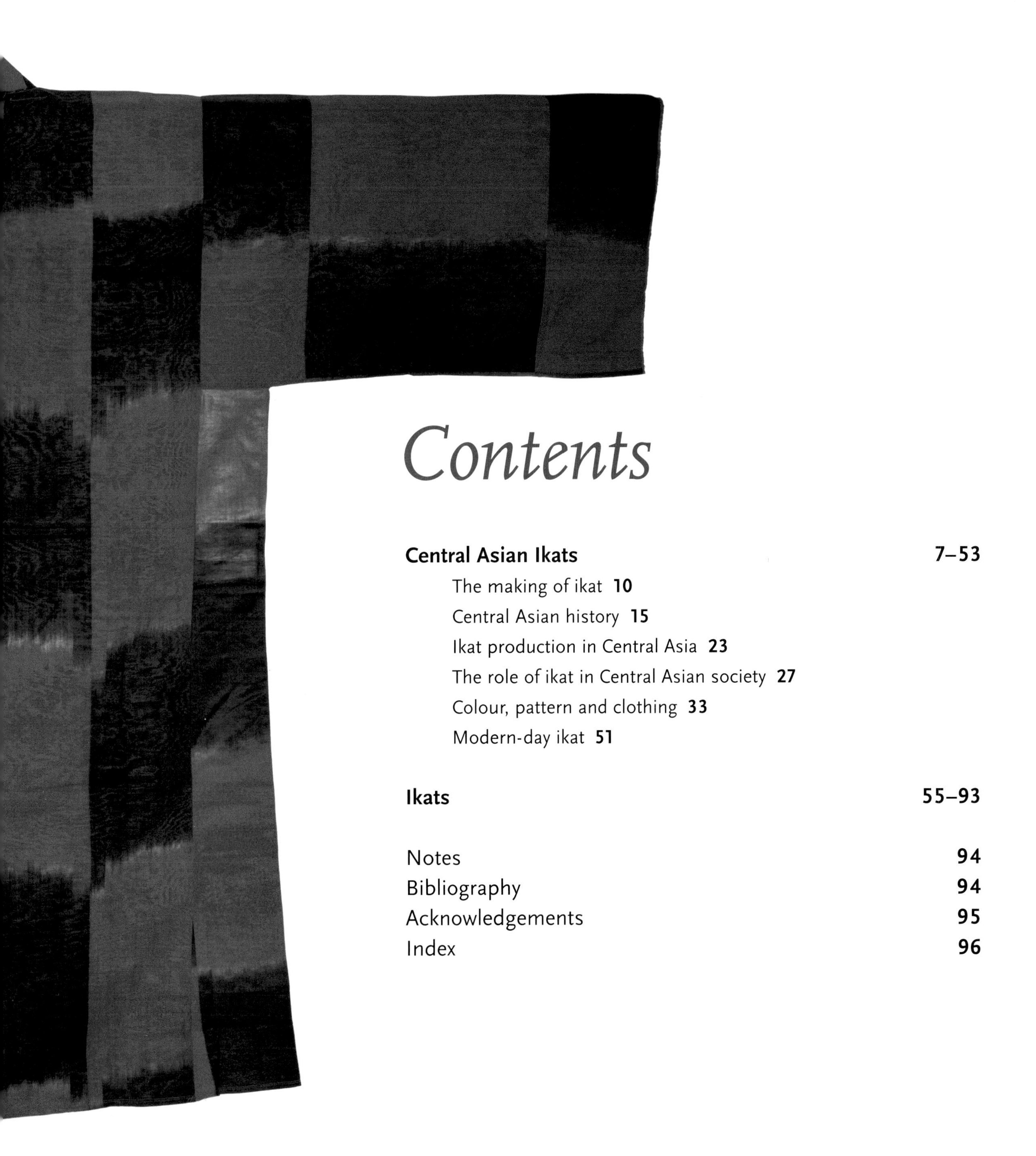

Contents

CENTRAL ASIAN IKATS

FROM THE RAU COLLECTION

THE textiles illustrated throughout this book – continually inventive in pattern and vivid in colour – are drawn from the collection of Doris (Pip) Rau in London. Rau's collection allows us a view of the extraordinary range of Central Asian ikats in the nineteenth century – the moment at which these textiles are often thought to have been at their finest in terms of design and technique, and certainly the period of their greatest popularity. Pip Rau first visited Afghanistan in 1974, reaching as far as Herat on this visit. She bought her first ikat textile in 1976 in Kabul, and went on to build her collection over numerous trips to Central Asia in the 1970s and 1980s. Most of her collecting was done in Afghanistan, where she gathered a superb selection of ikats from dealers and bazaars.

During the nineteenth century the countries of Central Asia underwent a period of sustained economic and cultural revival, and the golden age of ikat making was closely bound up with this new social dynamism. As so often in history, the making and marketing of textiles accompanied the founding, or expansion, of cities. Great centres across Central Asia, such as Samarkand and Bukhara in modern-day Uzbekistan, and Kabul and Kunduz in Afghanistan, became large and prosperous enough to develop whole neighbourhoods in which to house the dyers, weavers, binders and designers whose collaborative activity went into the making of the new fabrics.

Ikats were put to two main kinds of social use. They were shaped into more or less elaborate personal costumes, or, suitably enlarged, employed as hangings within the home. Hence they became crucial indicators of social power. Richness and originality of design, especially in a person's ceremonial robes, came to be a key marker of status, age and social dignity. Naturally, courts took a leading role; ikats became a preferred item of diplomatic gift-giving, with especially sumptuous and intricate examples exchanged between rulers and honoured guests.

Two elements are central to the appeal of the ikat to collectors and art-lovers: the sheer vibrancy and imaginativeness of their designs, and the clues they provide to the everyday life of the great region to which they belong. They are distinctive nineteenth-century creations, full of unmistakable urban energy, but they are also the product of a culture in which the making of textiles had been, for many centuries, a treasured and highly skilled speciality. The making and trading of fine fabrics had been one of Central Asia's chief economic activities since the beginnings of the Silk Road, and through the long period of Islamic dominance crucial skills and standards of judgment were preserved. Ikats reach back to an unparalleled textile tradition.

High-ranking dignitary in Bukhara, c.1900.
Museum für Völkerkunde, Vienna

OPPOSITE Wall hanging (detail). Silk and cotton, backed with printed cotton. 194 x 165cm
ABOVE Woman's robe. Silk and cotton, lined with printed cotton. 135 x 184.5cm

The making of ikat

THE term 'ikat' comes from the Malay word *mengikat*, meaning to tie or to bind. This refers to the tie-dyeing method used to give these textiles their unique vibrancy of colour and design. Ikat has now come to refer to the textiles themselves as well as the process.

The following description of the way Central Asian ikats are made is specific to current ikat production at Marghilan in Uzbekistan. The workshop there continues to use traditional inherited methods and so provides a good understanding of how the illustrated ikats were made; there would have been slight differences of method according to the location and the scale of production. The following method is also specific to warp ikat and would differ for weft or double ikat.

The first stage of making an ikat textile was making the silk thread. This was done by putting the cocoons into a pot of boiling water in order to kill the caterpillar and to dissolve the sericin, a kind of glue which binds the threads together inside the cocoon. The released silk filaments were then extracted using a stick or brush to catch the ends and wound by hand into skeins, directly from the pot. The resulting threads would have been of very uneven quality and were further refined, evened out and strengthened by winding them onto a hand-turned frame or spool and by repeatedly boiling the threads to increase whiteness and strength. The threads were then reeled onto bobbins ready to spin the warp threads (the warp threads are the lengthwise threads as the textile is woven; the wefts are the horizontal threads). A vertical frame holding several bobbins would feed threads onto a very large spinning wheel, with a circumference of 6.75 metres, to start the process of stretching out the threads to their full length. This could be up to 200 metres long.

Once they had been fully prepared – stretched, strengthened and divided into warp lengths – the threads went to the ikat binding workshop (*abr-bandi*) where they were separated into even groups, called *livits*, and threaded through between 40 and 60 holes pierced into the ends of a large wooden patterning frame. Once the warp was laid out in this way the designer marked out the pattern directly onto the threads using charcoal. He would draw the outline and indicate the areas intended for each colour.

Grabbing silk filament ends from a pot of boiling cocoons

Threads wound onto a turning frame to strengthen and even them out

Reeling the bobbins of silk

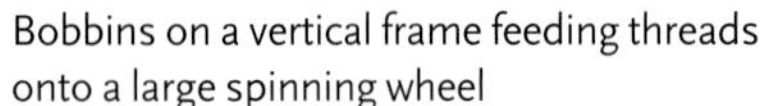
Bobbins on a vertical frame feeding threads onto a large spinning wheel

Warp threads on the patterning frame ready to be marked out for dyeing

Partially dyed warp threads with areas bound in preparation for next dye bath

The next stage was to bind the areas of the threads that were to resist the dye of the first dye bath. These areas were wrapped tightly with cotton threads so that the appropriately marked areas of the warp would resist the dye according to the design pattern. A water-repellent, usually wax, was also added at this stage to ensure that the tied areas remained undyed. The whole of the warp was then removed from its frame and sent to the dye house for its first application of colour. There, the threads were wrapped loosely around a long pole and immersed into a dye bath. This dyeing and binding process was extremely complex. For a multi-coloured ikat, reds and yellows tended to be applied first with a hot dye bath. These colours were applied in separate workshops to those in which the indigo dye was applied with a cold dye bath. The Tajiks tended to work the hot baths while the Jewish population, or Chala Muslims (converted Jews), worked with the indigo dyes. Additional colours were also added to a multi-coloured ikat by over-dyeing one colour with another.

After each dye was applied, the threads were wrung out by hand and returned to the *abr-bandi*, where the tied areas of the warp were unbound. They were then fixed to the patterning frame once again and the next area marked out for a particular colour was tied. In the more complex ikats, this process would be repeated several times, passing repeatedly between the designers and binders and the various dyeing workshops. It was a process of great skill and cooperation.

The dyes used for ikat were extracted from a variety of natural resources. The red came from the cochineal insect or from madder; green came from the seedpods and flowers of the pagoda tree or by dyeing yellow onto blue; yellow was made from delphinium, saffron or larkspur, and the pinks from Brazilwood; black dye was made from

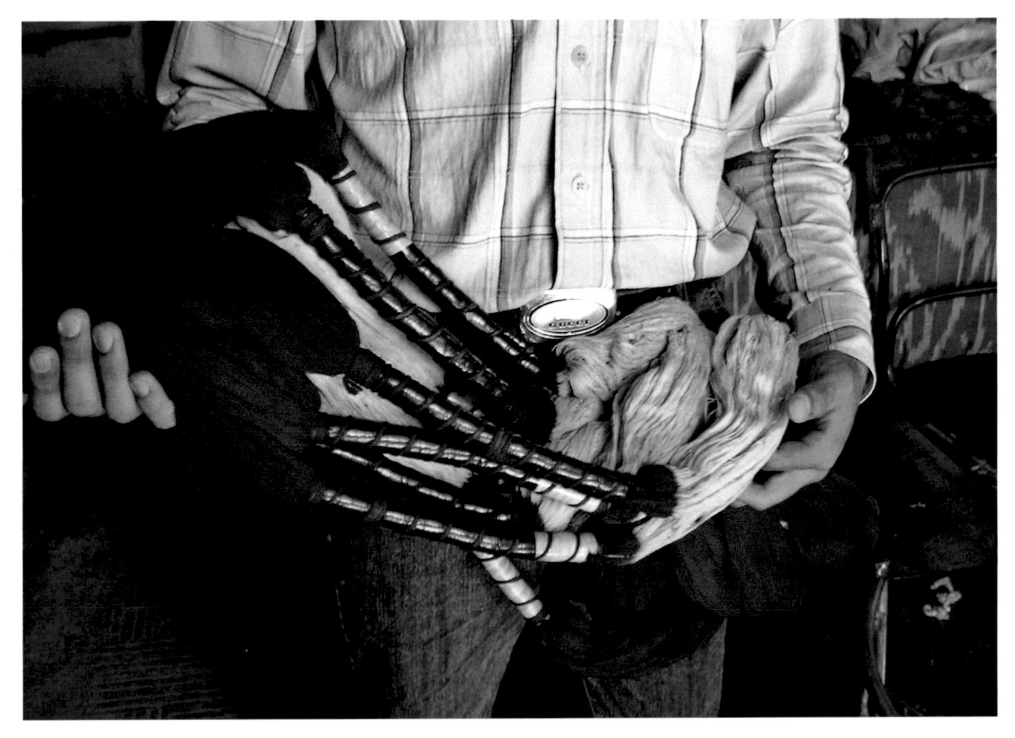

Warp bundles bound ready for second dye bath

Weaving a warp ikat

the skins of pomegranates, the black mallow plant or the galls of pistachio trees; and indigo from the indigo plant imported from India. The Jewish population was largely responsible for the import and trade of the textile dyes that were not available locally. Towards the end of the nineteenth century, synthetic dyes were widely used, taking the place of the labour-intensive traditional methods. The dyeing skills were never entirely lost though, and are still being practised today.

Once all the dyes were applied to the ikat warp, the threads were once again returned to the *abr-bandi* and unbound for the final time, and the warp was then sent to the weaving workshop. There the warp was cut into shorter lengths ready for weaving. The warp was then attached to a simple treadle loom (a loom in which pedals move the warps so that the wefts can be passed through). Central Asian ikats are warp-faced textiles, which means that the warp is much denser than the weft. The pattern of the warp is therefore not interrupted by the weft so the work of the designers, binders and dyers is visible to full effect. This also means that the weaving process is shorter and less complex than it might otherwise be.

The final stage was to apply a finish to the surface of the textile to give it its distinctive shiny surface. This was achieved by various methods. An egg-white solution, or a type of glue, was sometimes applied to the surface of the cloth. It was then beaten with a convex wooden hammer or a glass sphere which would soften the surface again. These tools also gave the slight rippled effect to the final shiny surface. Alternatively, no finishing solution was applied but the cloth was beaten in this same way. This released the natural oils of the silk threads, consequently providing a natural shine to the textile surface.

Central Asian history

OPPOSITE Ikat fragment of seven colours (*Haft Rang*). Silk and cotton, backed with printed cotton. 77.6 x 56cm

THE five independent states of modern-day Central Asia are Kazakhstan, Uzbekistan, Kyrgyzstan, Tajikistan and Turkmenistan. The area referred to as Central Asia has changed over time and according to political rule, but can be generally defined by its natural borders. The Caspian Sea borders its western edge, and it reaches the Hindu Kush, Pamir and Tian shan mountain ranges at its south and east. The north is bordered by the southern extent of the Ural Mountains at the west and the Altai Range at the east; the plains of Siberia lie in between. It also meets the great deserts of Iran – the Dasht-i Kavir and Dasht-i Lut – to the south-west.

The internal geography of Central Asia, the land that lies between the mountain ranges, consists of vast areas of desert and steppe interrupted and defined by river valleys, most notably those of the Amu and the Syr. This has meant that throughout its long history Central Asia has naturally fostered a population of on the one hand nomads, who moved through the steppes living off the land with grazing animals, and on the other oasis-dwellers, who have used the rivers to sustain cities and towns for thousands of years.

The geography of Central Asia thus has a great influence on its ways of life. Central Asia's internal geography dictates the distribution of its population, while its land-locked position has determined the important place that it has always occupied in international trade. Central Asia meets China and Mongolia in the east, India and Iran in the south, and Russia to the north. It has benefited greatly from occupying this trade bridge between Europe and Asia, although this has also made it vulnerable to attack from many sides throughout its history. The Silk Road, which crosses Central Asia, refers to a network of land routes used for the transportation of goods between the civilizations of east and west and has played an important part in Central Asian life and economy. The earliest evidence of this route being used to transport textiles is from a stone relief in Persepolis in Iran made during Sogdian rule in Central Asia. The stone carving shows merchants taking fabric to Persia in the sixth and fifth centuries BCE.[1]

The diverse ethnic mix of the population of Central Asia has also been a defining characteristic of its culture and artistic practice. Turkic peoples from many different clans and tribes dominated Central Asia until the Arab invasions; by the late seventh century Turkic khanates controlled many key trade cities stretching from Mongolia in the east to the Black Sea in the west. The Chinese had also conquered parts of Central Asia in the seventh century, and China's presence in Central Asia and at its border was significant in the emergence of trade as a major activity, especially when use of the Silk Road was at its peak. Luxury goods from as far away as Byzantium were able to flow in and out of China along the Silk Road.

From the year 709 CE, Central Asia was conquered by Arabs. Islam became the major religion within a few generations and Islamic culture became one of the dominant elements in Central Asian society from this point on, although it was always entwined with older local traditions and the many external influences that had passed through this area.

Nomadic horsemen lived in the vast areas of steppe land for hundreds of years, and there is a long history of conflict between them and the settled peoples. One of the many nomadic tribes was the Mongols, whose invasions in 1219 led by Genghis Khan ravaged huge areas and conquered a vast empire which included China, Korea, India, the Russian steppes, most of the Arab world and all of Central Asia. Under the rule of Genghis Khan, the Silk Road thrived for a while. He encouraged trade and made routes safe for travellers, including the most famous Western traveller to the Silk Road, the Venetian merchant Marco Polo (1254–1324). Central Asia was now at the heart of a huge empire and benefited from the arts and aesthetic influences of these disparate cultures grouped under the Mongols. Trade flourished throughout these vast lands for a time, but eventually civil wars and internal division among the Mongols saw this diminish.

Mongol rule ended with the rise of Tamerlane (Timur Leng) at the end of the fourteenth century. He founded the Timurid dynasty with Samarkand as its capital; many of the great monuments of Timurid architecture still stand today. After Tamerlane's death, a group of Turkish tribes that were already present in these lands, the Uzbeks, came into their own. The Uzbeks went on to dominate a long period of Central Asian history, up to and including the time of the making of the Rau ikats in the nineteenth century.

These moments in Central Asia are representative of its tumultuous history as a whole.

Robe. Silk and cotton, lined with printed cotton. 124 x 157cm

Its trade-based economy and internal stability went through a series of rises and falls according to the politics and strength of its rulers, and the successes of its invaders.

The importance of the Silk Road in the history of Central Asia should not be understated. From as early as the fifth or sixth centuries BCE right through to the discovery of sea routes by the Portuguese, merchandise passing to and from East Asia and the Mediterranean travelled through the oasis towns of Central Asia along the Silk Road. The route was not only used for silks but for many kinds of trade goods. Gold and other precious metals, ivory, precious stones and glass were all transported from west to east along these routes, while furs, ceramics, jade, bronze, lacquer and iron were traded in the other direction. Cities such as Bukhara and Samarkand benefited greatly from their position as a crossroads for this exchange of goods, techniques and ideas.

The movement of textiles in particular, and the exchange of techniques that travelled with them, brought the relevant expertise to Central Asia and helped to encourage the local traditions that meant textile production became its major industry. The designers and makers of nineteenth-century ikats drew on the ancient motifs that originated locally as well as those that had travelled in at some time in the Silk Road's history. Motifs such as rams' horns and scorpions appeared in very early Central Asian art and still appear in ikats of the nineteenth century.

Though the opening of sea routes eventually led to its decline, the centuries during which the Silk Road thrived had meant that Central Asian populations were focused on trade, and especially on the trade of textiles. Central Asian cities continued to flourish and to produce some of the world's most impressive textiles.

The end of the Silk Road did mark the start of a much more introspective culture for Central Asia, and certainly it was a much more isolated part of the world from the sixteenth century onwards. The Shaibanids, ruling over a largely Uzbek population, fell foul of internal rivalries and fighting with nomadic tribes. Their successors, the Janid dynasty (1599–1784), took Bukhara as their capital and saw the founding of the three khanates of Khiva, Kokand and Bukhara. This dynasty broke up after the death of its leader, Abd al-Aziz Khan, led to more internal wrangling. Under the Manjit dynasty (1757–1920), Bukhara found economic prosperity as an important centre for trade. It was also home to a booming textile industry built on the many skills of its diverse population, which included Uzbeks, Tajiks, Arabs, Turkmen, Kazakhs, Kyrgiz, immigrants from Merv in Turkmenistan, as well as a significant Jewish community.

From the middle of the nineteenth century Russia gained control of large parts of Central Asia. Bukhara became part of the Russian Empire in 1868, although it maintained its industries for several years after that. It was officially incorporated into the Soviet Union with the Russian revolution in 1917 and became the Bukharan People's Soviet Republic in 1920.

This description of the history of Central Asia shows how turbulent it has been at various times. The economy was often unstable but also sometimes booming; there was a long history of internal warfare as well as invasion from outside. It is the case though that most of its ruling dynasties had an interest in encouraging trade, spurred on by a desire to continue the history of the Silk Road.

OPPOSITE Turkmen women in Khiva, c.1890. Museum für Völkerkunde, Vienna

Jewish family in Bukhara, c.1900. Museum für Völkerkunde, Vienna

A young Uzbek woman in Samarkand. From Krafft, *A travers le Turkestan russe* (Paris, 1902), p.150

Ikat production in Central Asia

OPPOSITE Woman's robe. Silk and cotton, lined with printed cotton. 125.5 x 168cm

VARIOUS circumstances allowed ikat production in nineteenth-century Central Asia to thrive, but we know little about what exactly prompted its beginning. The origins of the ikat technique are a matter of scholarly debate and uncertainty. The earliest surviving piece of ikat was found in Japan and dates from the Asuka period (552–644 CE), and is now in the Tokyo National Museum. On a mostly aesthetic basis, it has been suggested that this piece is of Central Asian origin.[2] Other early evidence comes from the Ajanta cave paintings in India which date from the fifth to seventh centuries and depict people who appear to be wearing ikat cloth. The technique is also known to have been practised in China, India, the Yemen and Egypt by at least the seventh century. No early pieces of Central Asian ikat have been excavated and there is no evidence of the technique being practised there until the early years of the nineteenth century. It is not known for certain whether the technique was inherited from India or China, or if in fact it had been practised in Central Asia through the centuries.

It is equally not certain at what date silk was first produced locally. Silk production was invented in China in 3000 BCE and the technique kept secret for centuries. From 1000 BCE, Central Asian silk textiles were made from imported Chinese threads that came along the Silk Road. Eventually, perhaps as early as the second century CE, they cultivated their own silkworms to make silk threads.

Although there is no excavated evidence of ikat being made in this area before the nineteenth century, considering the history of skilled textile production in Central Asia and the zeal and skill with which the technique was practised in the nineteenth century, it seems unlikely that this ancient technique took quite so long to reach Central Asia.

By the middle of the seventeenth century, the prosperity that the Silk Road had created was diminishing. Industrialization and with it improved transport methods meant that Silk Road cities lost their significance to world trade. In response to this decline, the region focused its attentions internally and broke up into several localized political entities, such as the Khanates of Khiva, Kokand, Bukhara in Uzbekistan, and

Sarts (urban Persian speakers) weaving ikat, c.1900

Kunduz in northern Afghanistan. While the fracturing of these lands led to some instabilities, it also resulted in a revival of regional industries and crafts.

Although Central Asia became less economically powerful in the seventeenth and eighteenth centuries, its geographical position ensured that it always remained of some strategic value to the new trading nations of the world. On a local level the khanate of Bukhara especially entered a period of relative prosperity and stability by the nineteenth century, acting as a central market place for the trade of goods within the emirate, and also for trade goods needed outside Central Asia.

It is most likely that when this moment of ikat making began in Central Asia it was in Bukhara in the early nineteenth century. More than any other town in the area it had all the necessary elements to support such an industry, and as such is often taken as a case study to describe general trends in the ikat production of the area. All the raw materials needed to produce ikat were locally available, and throughout its history Bukhara had acquired a great expertise for textile production thanks to its central position along the Silk Road. Skilled artisans were attracted there because of its long association with textile making and good trade connections, and they in turn brought their own expertise. By the nineteenth century Bukhara had all the textile workers needed to facilitate ikat production. There were dyers, weavers, designers, silk spinners, and the wealth of Bukhara's upper class created a market for these impressive fabrics.

Samarkand became an important centre for ikat production a little later in the nineteenth century. It was also made in the Ferghana Valley at Marghilan and at oasis towns in northern Afghanistan. The technique seems to have been practised in all of the Uzbek khanates. Such was ikat's importance, when Yakub Beg, commander-in-chief of the army of the Khanate of Kokand, appointed himself ruler of Kashgaria in north-western China, initially ruling as vassal to the Khan of Kokand, he took with him the skilled workers needed to produce the fine ikat cloths of the khanates that he would use to adorn the luxury of his court.

OPPOSITE Ikat length (detail). Silk and cotton with glaze. Before 1870. 28.5 x 614cm. V&A: 7941(IS)

It is important to understand the range of people involved in producing ikats. Various different groups and workshops worked together to complete each fabric. The dyers occupied one neighbourhood, the weavers another, and the threads were passed from place to place to reach completion. The separation of areas according to skill also tended to coincide with ethnic divisions. The trade in dyes used for ikats tended to be controlled by the Jewish or Chala Muslim population, while the dyeing itself was done by low-status social groups as it was seen as an unpleasant, smelly and messy job. Women were largely active in the home and not in the market place or workshops; they would raise silk worm and spin yarn that could be used for ikat making.

Of all the groups working on making ikat, the weavers were the most numerous, and the most regulated. Weaving workshops were governed by the Weaver's Guild, set up in Bukhara in the nineteenth century in order to protect workers and regulate the market. Some 50 neighbourhoods in Bukhara were occupied by weavers, so the creation of this body was important. The Guild defined relationships between master craftsmen and their workers. The apprentices, of which there were from one or two up to twenty in the houses of the master craftsmen, got paid according to how many textiles they produced. The Guild ensured they were fairly treated and did not behave badly, and settled any disputes between the master and apprentice. Importantly, the Guild also set prices for the textiles produced in the very numerous houses.

The role of ikat in Central Asian society

OPPOSITE Ikat length (detail). Silk velvet. 67.8 x 128cm. V&A: T.30–1930

DURING the nineteenth century Central Asia attracted a number of travellers from Europe and Russia, whose photographs and writings describe the prominence of ikat textiles in this society. Not only do they show us the widespread use of these textiles throughout Central Asia, but also provide descriptions of the use of fine ikats as gifts to thank or honour guests. This tradition of exchanging robes of honour (*khil'ats*) goes far back into Asian history. The ceremony consists of a ruler presenting fine robes, usually made of silk, to their honoured visitors before an audience. The status of fine quality silks was very high.

One traveller to Central Asia was the English tea-planter Robert Shaw (1839–79), who travelled from northern India to Central Asia in 1868–9 at a time when Russia and Britain were vying for control of Central Asia. He recorded the details of his trip to visit the ruler of Kashgaria, Yakub Beg, in his book *Visits to the High Tartary, Yârkand and Kâshgar.*[3] Yakub Beg's rule in Kashgar was established under the umbrella of the khanate of Kokand, and had brought with it many of the traditional crafts of Kokand, inheriting its artistic practices and skilled craftsmen.

As the first English traveller to these parts of the Silk Road, Shaw's account of his trip to cities such as Yarkand and Kashgar is a valuable and engaging resource. Shaw mentions being given robes of honour on several occasions. During Shaw's journey to Yarkand, great honours were paid to him as a guest of the 'king', by way of 'honouring the English nation in one of its members'.[4] He was accompanied on his route by his own companion, called his Yookbashee ('head of luggage'), as well as other servants and a steady stream of messengers going back and forth to Yarkand to tell the Shaghawal (governor) of his visitor's progress. At the approach to Yarkand, Shaw is informed that he will be met by 'some person of consequence, either the brother or son of the Shaghawal, to whom it would be proper to present a "jâma", or robe'.[5] It was decided that Shaw did not have a good enough robe to present to such a person so the messengers sent word that he should be met by someone less important. He did present this man with a robe which had been lent to him by his companion, but it was obviously not one of appropriate quality for the more superior relation

LEFT Member of the ruling family of Kuliab with his son in Bukhara, 1890. Museum für Völkerkunde, Vienna
OPPOSITE Man's robe. Silk and cotton, lined with printed cotton. 116 x 152.5cm

of the Shaghawal that may have greeted him.[6] This interesting negotiation reveals the place that quality textiles had in court life, and the status they endowed.

When Shaw visits the Shaghawal himself, he is presented with a 'rich silk robe' which is placed on his shoulders as he takes his leave. This ritual of gift-giving to honour the visitor is described more than once in the subsequent text. A long robe of crimson silk is sent to Shaw's accommodation, and the Shaghawal presents him with yet another robe at their final meeting.

When Shaw arrives at his destination of Kashgar there is also a long description of gift-giving to 'the king'. His visit with Yakub Beg ends with a pink satin robe being placed onto Shaw's shoulders before he is graciously dismissed.[7]

Ruth Barnes has identified that some of the robes Shaw describes are now held in the collection at the Ashmolean Museum in Oxford.[8] This collection includes several splendid ikat

khil'ats which were presented to Shaw on his journey. Although Shaw does not use the term ikat, it is certain that many of the robes he was given during his visit were of fine ikat cloth.

This example of the relationship between textiles and social status has many other parallels in Central Asian history. Textiles had special status in the Islamic world, and the quality of an individual's clothes signified their place in society. Gifts of lavish clothing were also given as thanks or reward by those in power; these robes of honour would in turn themselves define the status of the recipient.

Ikat was popular at the highest levels of society, with some high-ranking officials wearing up to ten robes at once according to their wealth and status. It also became more widely popular at every level of society and played an important role in family rituals. Textile hangings would have adorned the walls of Central Asian mud-brick houses, and these would sometimes include sections of ikat. In poorer families, ikat textiles were reserved for special uses, where textiles had always played a part. Ikat cloth wrapped newborn babies; they were an important part of a dowry; they were worn at weddings and by widows in mourning. None of the cloth was wasted: smaller sections of ikat would sometimes be sewn into blankets or made into children's clothes.

The poorer population mostly wore locally woven cotton clothing; the next level up would be *adras* cloth, which has a silk warp and a cotton weft, followed by the all-silk warp and weft known as *abr* (cloud in Persian). The most sumptuous and expensive ikat worn by the highest rank was silk-velvet ikat, called *baghmal*, sometimes adorned with gold embroidery. There were sumptuary laws that meant you were punished for wearing a robe indicating a higher status than your own.

ABOVE Tax collectors from Shirabad, Bukhara, 1890. Museum für Völkerkunde, Vienna
OPPOSITE Woman and child, Bukhara or Samarkand, late 19th century

Colour, pattern and clothing

OPPOSITE FAR LEFT Ikat length (detail). Silk velvet. 134.2 x 35.5cm. V&A: IS 2819–1883
OPPOSITE LEFT Ikat length (detail). Silk velvet. 285 x 35.5cm. V&A: 2145(IS)

AS well as the richness of the material of ikat costume varying according to the status and wealth of its owner, it has also been asserted that patterns and colours varied according to region, gender and date. While some general variations do exist and are worth identifying, attempts to establish a firm chronology of these textiles cannot be reliably based on such differences. Very few ikats can be reliably dated, and it is only possible to note very general trends of particular colour preferences in certain areas at certain times. The market for ikat demanded rich, bold colours, striking patterns and quality silk production. It is not helpful to our understanding of the historical context they were made in to look for deeper meaning in their choices of colour and design, or even to hope that we can date them exactly.

The earliest dated ikats in the UK are from the Shaw collection at the Ashmolean Museum, which are known to date from before 1868. The Victoria and Albert Museum's collection of lengths of ikat fabrics was received in 1880 from the India Museum. Documentation handed over with them record that they were purchased on two separate occasions, the first group in Kabul in 1870 and the second in Yarkand in April 1875. We can therefore date these textiles prior to these acquisition years (see pages 84 to 93). The fact that these pieces were bought as new at point of purchase also suggests that was likely to have been the place in which they were made. The colour and design range of the V&A pieces is wide and includes several velvet ikats. Velvet ikat seems only to have been produced for a relatively short time span in the nineteenth century, possibly from the 1860s until the end of the century, which ties in with the dating of the V&A pieces.

In this study, no attempt has been made to pinpoint the date or place of production of individual pieces to anything more specific than nineteenth-century Central Asia in almost all cases. This approach acknowledges the difficulties in attempting to assign exact place and date to these textiles based on what might be small stylistic variations, and instead stresses the fact that ikat was being made from Bukhara to Kabul to Kashgar to similarly excellent standards for similar audiences throughout the nineteenth century.

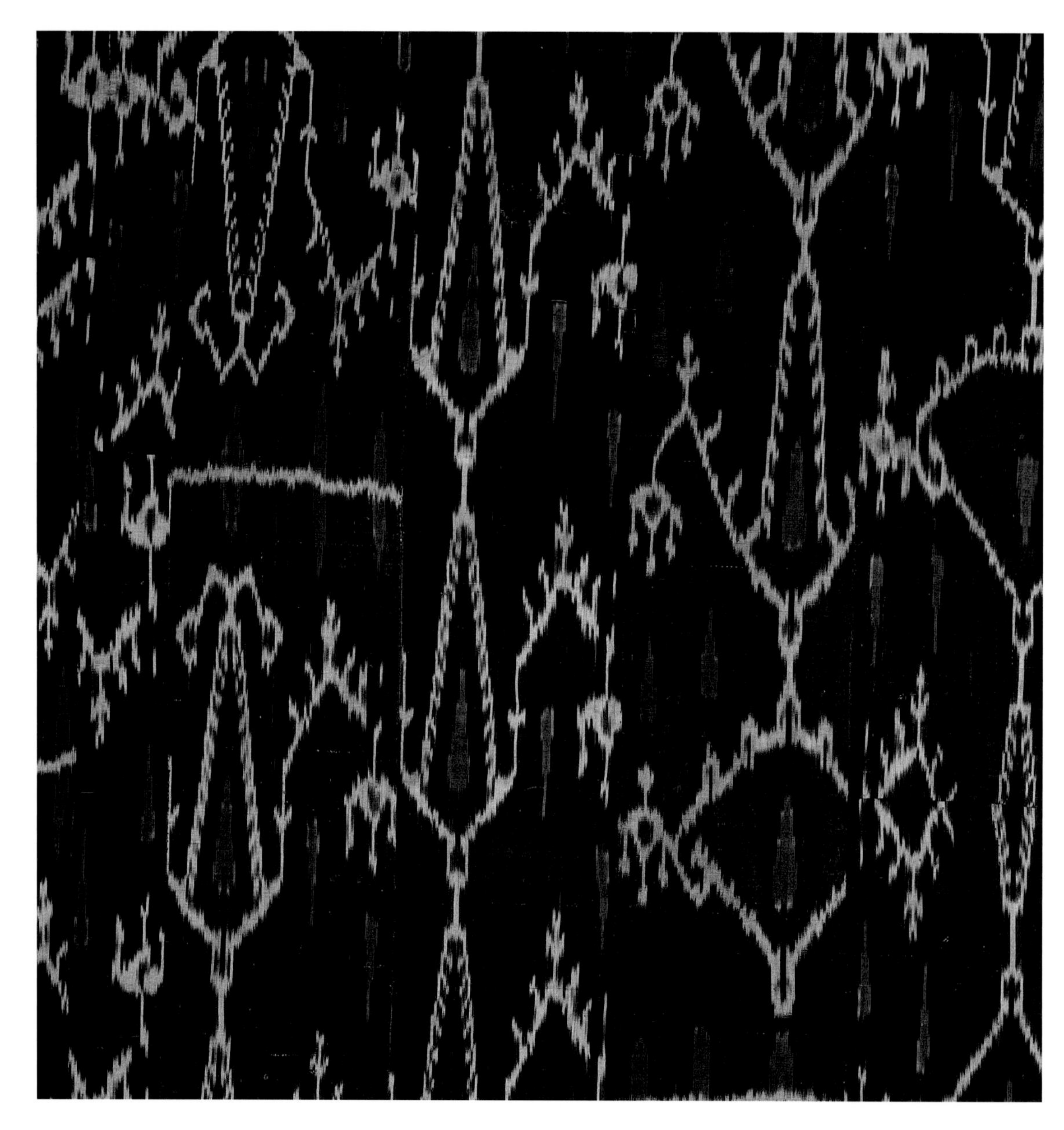

The colours of ikat textiles are their most important feature. It is the range and depth of the colours that draws the local population to appreciate the ikats of this period; there was a traceable historical taste for bright, vibrantly coloured fabrics. It is true that certain regions preferred particular colour schemes, that women tended to wear the most elaborately colourful pieces, and that older people wore the more sombre darker shades, also worn by those in mourning. It has been observed that ikat dyers in Bukhara used lots of claret-red, yellow, pink and blue, while in the Ferghana Valley they had a wider colour range, producing fine ikats of seven colours (*Haft Rang*), often with golden yellow as the main colour.

In their extensive study of the subject, Kate Fitz Gibbon and Andrew Hale have noted that the evidence of the many ethnographic photographs taken in the nineteenth century shows the

ABOVE LEFT Wall hanging (detail).
Silk and cotton, backed with printed cotton.
136 x 89.5cm
ABOVE CENTRE Wall hanging (detail).
Silk and cotton, backed with printed cotton.
206.5 x 145cm
ABOVE RIGHT Wall hanging (detail).
Silk and cotton, backed with printed cotton.
197 x 127.5cm

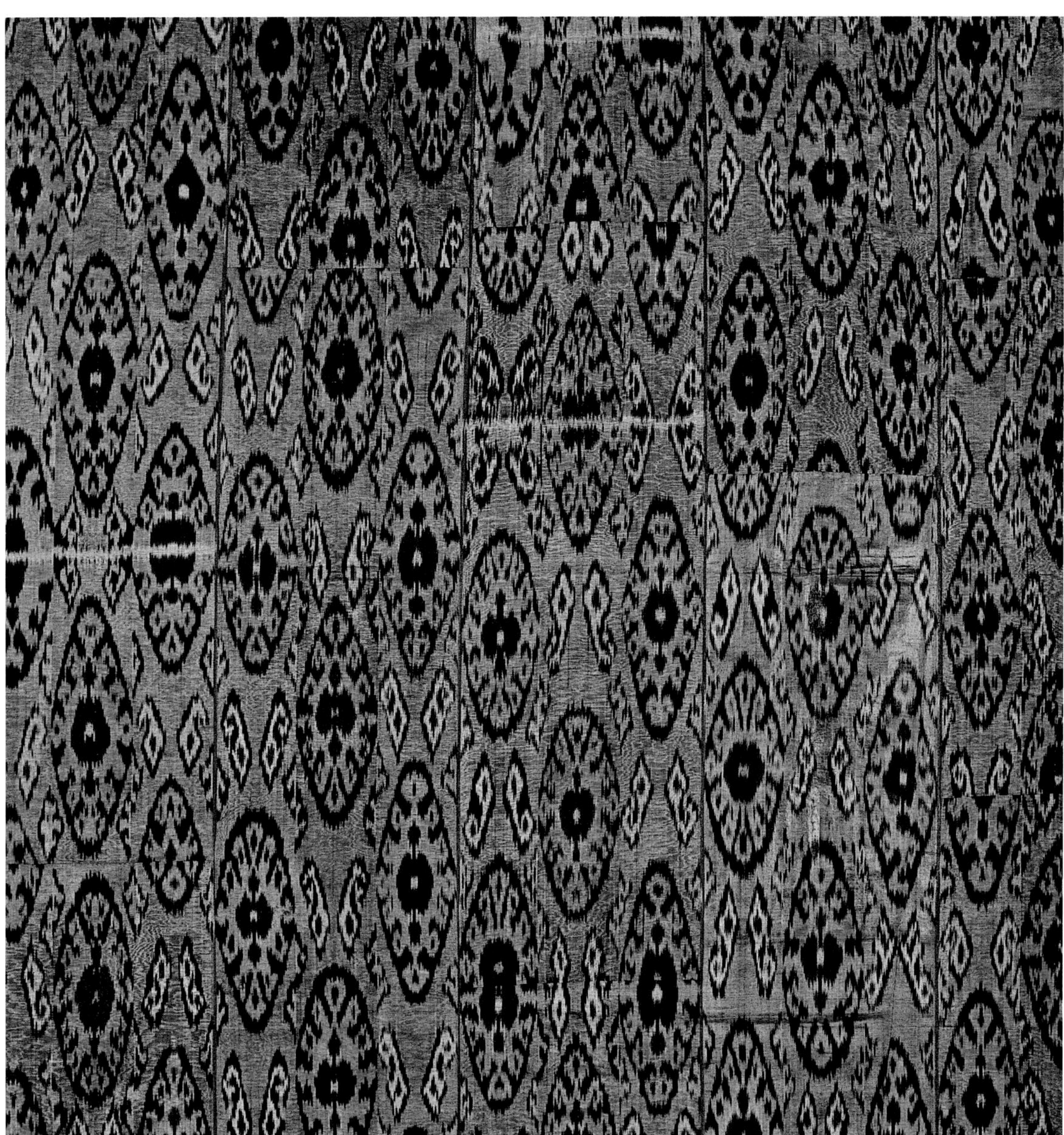

widespread popularity of ikat. The authors also show that a wide range of designs were popular simultaneously and that tastes for particular designs and colours did not change much until the last decades of the century.[9] They do go on to identify certain chronologies of ikat colours and designs, however. The earliest ikats tend to be complex patterns using many colours, and of a very fine technique. After the middle of the century a much greater range of designs was produced in rich but fewer colours; indigo fabrics with delicate patterns were probably introduced around this time but were still being produced until the end of the century.[10] Ikat production probably began in the Ferghana valley from the middle of the century, and the pattern of branching horns from a central stem could have originated in this area, but becomes more widespread later. An unusual palette has also been noted in Ferghana, including a striking bright green.

Man's robe. Silk and cotton, lined with printed cotton. After 1900. 147 x 220cm

The most obvious shift in taste for colour and pattern is seen in the later ikats. In the last two decades of the century the palette was reduced in number, with many ikats being produced in only two or three colours. Ikat patterns became large and simplified, and blocks of bright, shocking colours were used to fill the often geometric abstract designs. Part of the reason for the shift in tastes during the later decades of the century was the import of cheaper textiles and chemical dyes from Russia. The market had begun to demand less expensive textiles in-keeping with the prices of the new imports. Chemical dyes were easier to use and therefore less time consuming and the ikats became cheaper to produce.

There is great artistry in the arrangement of the colours in the finest ikats. The dyers' skill at achieving rich and bold saturated colours is combined with the designers' arrangement of

Man's robe. Silk and cotton, lined with printed cotton. After 1900. 146 x 217cm

colours to great effect. It is also worth looking in a little more detail at the range of patterns and motifs employed by the ikat designers, less to establish firm facts of chronology and varying tastes than to understand the range of influences they were responding to.

The designs on Central Asian ikats tend to be abstract overall surface patterns. The motifs that appear repeatedly are often part of a long-established local repertoire of designs, some of which were drawn from the other local textile traditions of carpet making and *suzanis* (large traditional embroidered wall hangings). A connection has been made between ikats with circle designs and *suzani* embroideries that also feature large circle patterns, while early ikats may have borrowed their overall mottled backgrounds from local carpet patterns.[11]

Other motifs used on ikats can be divided into a number of types. The oasis towns that

produced the ikats had daily interaction with the inhabitants of the steppe and with that land, and this influence is seen in the repeated use of the imagery of nature. A pattern of pine cones, or *boteh*, are often represented (the Farsi word '*boteh*' means flower but has been interpreted as pine cone, pear tree, flame or tear drop). This pattern came to Britain on shawls from Kashmir and the design was then copied by shawl weavers in Europe, including those in Paisley, the town which gives the pattern its British name. Other common patterns include cypress trees (see page 34), pomegranates and flowers.

Vegetal forms are also very common in much of the history of Islamic art. The forms of Islamic art that had been established over hundreds of years up to the time that these textiles were being made were an influence on those used to decorate the ikats; repetitive geometric patterns were an important design element. Ikat designers took up various forms from previous Islamic traditions and inherited the emphasis on abstract overall surface ornament.

There are certain other motifs that appear often. Rams' horns, scorpion tails and peacocks feature on many ikats, as they had been a part of the iconography of many Central Asian arts for centuries. Household items such as combs and water jugs also appear. The symbol of the *hamsa* – literally meaning 'five' in Arabic, and also referred to as the hand of Fatima (the daughter of the Prophet) – is used frequently, and represents the protective hand of God in both Jewish and Islamic iconography. Pendants and jewellery designs also feature.

ABOVE LEFT Woman's robe. Silk and cotton, lined with printed cotton. 126 x 173cm
ABOVE RIGHT Woman's coat. Silk and cotton, lined with printed cotton. 129 x 190cm
OPPOSITE Small wall hanging with rosettes and pomegranates (detail). Silk and cotton. 77 x 53cm

OPPOSITE Wall hanging (detail). Silk and cotton. 235 x 156cm
ABOVE Wall hanging. Silk and cotton, backed with printed cotton. 141.5 x 76cm
RIGHT Wall hanging. Silk and cotton, backed with printed cotton. 159 x 115.5cm

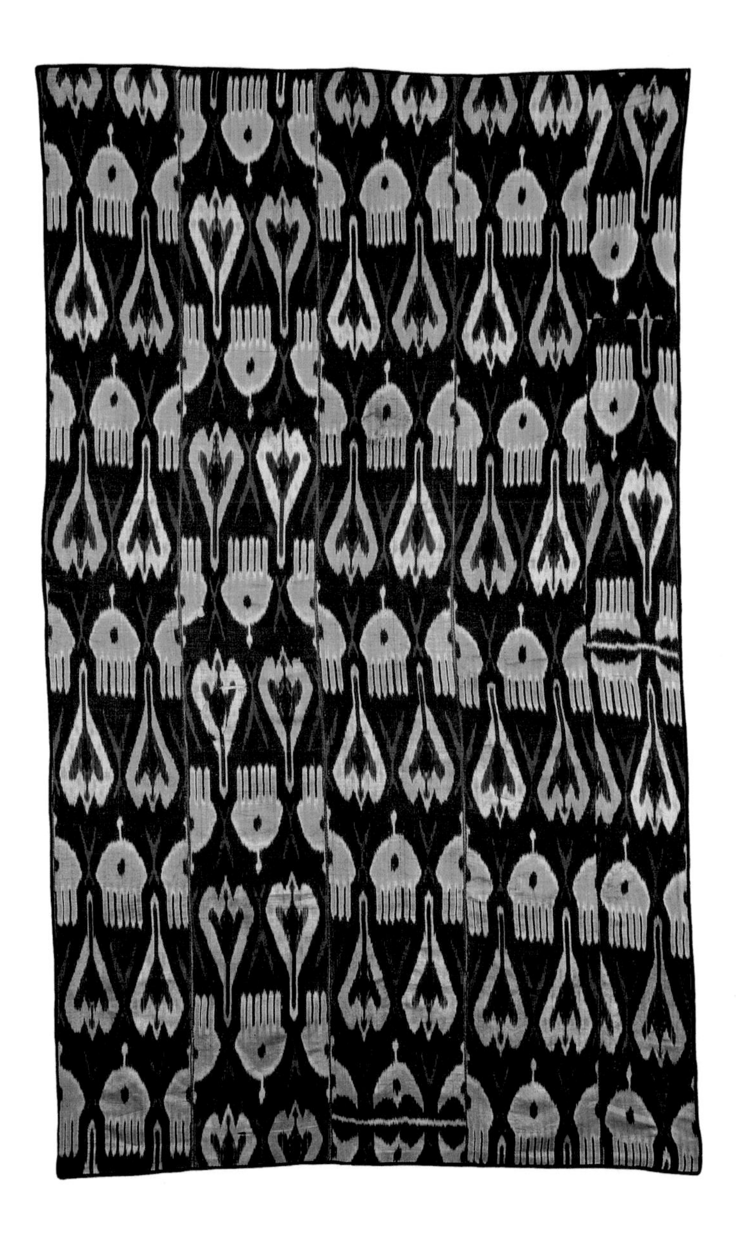

LEFT Wall hanging. Silk and cotton, backed with printed cotton. 217.5 x 167cm
ABOVE Wall hanging. Silk and cotton, backed with printed cotton. 230 x 133cm
OPPOSITE Wall hanging (detail). Silk and cotton, backed with printed cotton. 195 x 105cm

Certain designs have been attributed with amuletic or protective qualities in Islamic traditions or folklore. While this association was a fortuitous one, it is not the case that the robes then became talismans themselves. The designers were repeating imagery from their available vocabulary but they were without any special meaning. It is unproductive to try to attribute meaning to particular motifs or designs of these nineteenth-century Central Asian ikats. It is clear that the priority of the makers was first the combinations of colours merged together or set apart, and then an overall surface pattern, rather than individual elements. The patterns were drawn from the various influences of the steppe lands, of Islamic design and of ancient local motifs of Central Asian lands, which may have originated there or been brought in by the many traders or invaders along the Silk Road.

A great quantity of ikat was used for wall hangings. Panels of cloth of the same pattern were joined together in varying numbers; part of the aesthetic of these hangings is in the mismatched joins of the ikat lengths that were sewn together. The other significant use for ikat cloth was clothing. The traditional outfit at this time was an inner tunic, or *kurta*, worn over loose trousers with an overcoat or robe. This was the standard costume across all sections of society; the variations were found in quality of materials and details. When ikat could be afforded it was used for the outer garments so it was on show. All those that could afford silk garments wore them, certainly in the oasis towns. The robes were of an almost standard size, which meant they reached the mid-calf, and were very wide, so that they could be layered. Some of the wealthiest men would wear multiple robes layered on top of each other. The sleeves were often very long, to be worn hanging well below the hands. The man's overcoat, the *chapan* or *khalat*, was padded and lined, made from silk, half-silk or cotton. There were also lightweight robes, the *yaktak* or *degdeh*, and the *chakman*, a robe of heavy coarse cotton.

It has been suggested that Bukharan men wore the boldest and most colourful robes available to them, while men in Samarkand were more restrained in their choice of colour and pattern. The style of robes in Ferghana valley and Tashkent also tended to be more sober than those of Bukhara. Historians have identified differences in the cuts of robes from these locations, noting the extravagant width of Bukharan robes compared to the less flamboyant robes of

ABOVE LEFT An unidentified group, possibly from Bukhara, wearing a range of costumes. The central woman wears a *parandja* and the man next to her is wearing layered ikat robes.
ABOVE RIGHT Dancing boy and girl in Kokand, c.1890. Museum für Völkerkunde, Vienna
OPPOSITE Woman's robe. Silk and cotton with embroidered sleeves, lined with printed cotton. 137 x 123.5cm

OPPOSITE Woman's dress. Silk. 130 x 159cm
ABOVE LEFT Nomad woman on a yak, Bukharan countryside, c.1900
ABOVE RIGHT Dancing boys wearing ikat robes

Samarkand and Ferghana. Men often wore riding breeches with a pouch and a knife tucked into a sash or belt. These accessories, made in more or less lavish materials, varied according to social status and wealth. Men also wore a headdress of a cap wrapped with a turban.

Reliant as we are on the documentation of nineteenth-century Western travellers for information about life in the early part of this period, we do not know much about Central Asian Muslim women, as they mostly lived inside the home. There is more evidence regarding Jewish women and nomadic women. We learn more about women's clothing from later in the century. Women's robes can be differentiated from men's as they are gathered under the arms. Robes with a closed seam at the front were only worn by women. Married women had a long opening at the front of their robes for breast-feeding, while young girls' dresses had a small horizontal opening at the neck.

The *parandja* or *faranji* was also worn only by women. This robe was designed to be worn over the top of the head outside all other clothing. Often worn with a heavy veil, it would obscure the woman's features completely. These robes have fake sleeves that tie at the back so the woman's hands remained hidden inside the robe. The *parandja* tended to be quite a luxurious item and was only worn outside the home. Once again, there were variations in the fabrics of these robes according to where and when they were made and the age of the wearer. Darker colours were worn by older women or by widows. Another variation of women's clothing is the *munisak* robe that is gathered at both sides of the waist and shaped over the breast. The *munisak* was an important item in a woman's dowry and tended to be worn for family occasions, for weddings and funerals. Female headdresses also consisted of caps and scarves, sometimes adorned with jewellery.

Most ikat robes were lined with printed cotton fabrics imported from Persia, Russia or England. A strip of ikat was often added to the inside edge of the opening of the robe so that this was visible with the movement of the robe.

By the end of the nineteenth century Western influence was infiltrating Central Asian costume. Men made the transition first, but by 1930 Western styles of dress had become standard across the population, with tailored robes and dresses with collars, pockets and buttons all becoming standard.

RIGHT Woman's robe.
Silk and cotton. 121.5 x 160cm
OPPOSITE Woman's coat (*parandja*).
Cotton, lined with silk and cotton ikat. 159.5 x 290.5cm

Modern-day ikat

THE nineteenth century saw the heyday of ikat textile manufacture, but the history of the ikat does not stop abruptly in 1900 – modernization takes command. Once the Russian textile industry had infiltrated Central Asian markets – a process that was largely complete by the late 1800s – ikat producers were forced to respond to the new pressures. They adjusted initially by reducing the number of colours used and by simplifying patterns so as to reduce the cost for the consumer who could now buy cheaper factory-made fabrics. As the Russian products spread further into Central Asia, the market became more and more uniform and 'international', and in some instances local crafts died out altogether. The Russians were indefatigable; they needed the supply of cotton available in Central Asia, and they soon saw the potential of a vast new market in which they could sell their goods. Competition was often cut-throat: cheap printed textiles, produced in quantity using the latest factory techniques, were made to imitate ikat patterns, and aimed specifically – and often successfully – at consumers in Central Asian cities.

Another interesting offshoot of this was the run of porcelain plates with an ikat design that were made in the Gardner Factory in Russia. This factory was established in Verbilki, near Moscow, by an Englishman called Francis Gardner. The factory produced excellent quality porcelains for both popular and Imperial consumption, and was known for its floral designs. The factory also produced an unusual run of 'ikat' plates intended mostly for the Central Asian market. Examples of the plates were bought by travellers and collectors in the 1870s and 1880s in Afghanistan and brought back to this country. These examples of the re-use of ikat design are evidence of the lasting local tastes for the colours and designs that were produced so beautifully by the ikat makers of the nineteenth century. They are also part of an attempt by the Russians to make their newly expanding lands appear, if only visually, unified.

The world market for textiles goes on changing, and Central Asia is no exception. In recent years the production of ikat has been revived in some locations along the Silk Road. The traditional techniques of ikat making were

OPPOSITE Ikat length. Silk velvet. c.2005. 38 x 166cm. Private collection, London

never entirely lost: there is a continuous history of ikat production in Central Asia, which continues today in a number of workshops in which craftspeople are making ikat in the traditional way. There has been a concerted attempt to preserve and revive traditional skills serving the local market as well as that of tourism. In Marghilan in Uzbekistan ikat cloth is being made using the traditional method[12], while some impressive velvet ikats are again being made in Tashkent, using natural dyes and following age-old procedures. Textiles like these, it seems, are now being produced for a small but discerning market wanting hand-made designs of real originality and fine workmanship, both in Central Asia and around the world.

Ikat length. Silk velvet. c.2005. 33 x 67cm.
Private collection, London

Ikats

Wall hanging. Silk and cotton, backed with printed cotton. 220.5 x 151cm

Woman's robe. Silk and cotton, lined with printed cotton. 117 x 165cm

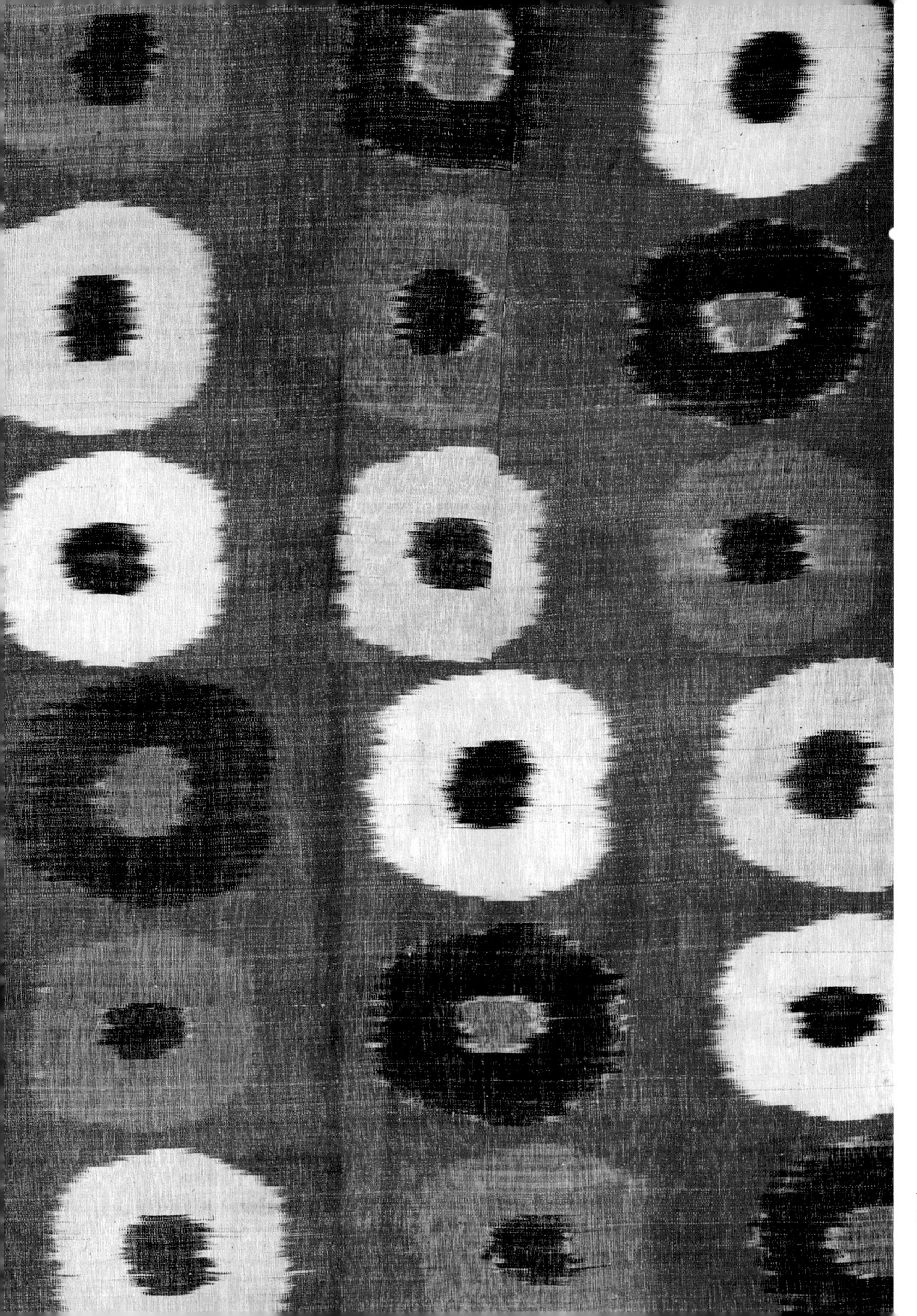

Wall hanging (detail). Silk and cotton, backed with cotton. 165.5 x 79cm

Ikat length. Silk velvet. 183 x 33cm

RIGHT Woman's robe. Silk and cotton, lined with printed cotton. 125.5 x 186cm
OPPOSITE Wall hanging. Silk and cotton, backed with printed cotton. 231 x 135.5cm

ABOVE Wall hanging. Silk and cotton, backed with printed cotton. 238 x 138cm
OPPOSITE Wall hanging (detail). Silk and cotton, backed with printed cotton. 247 x 151.5cm

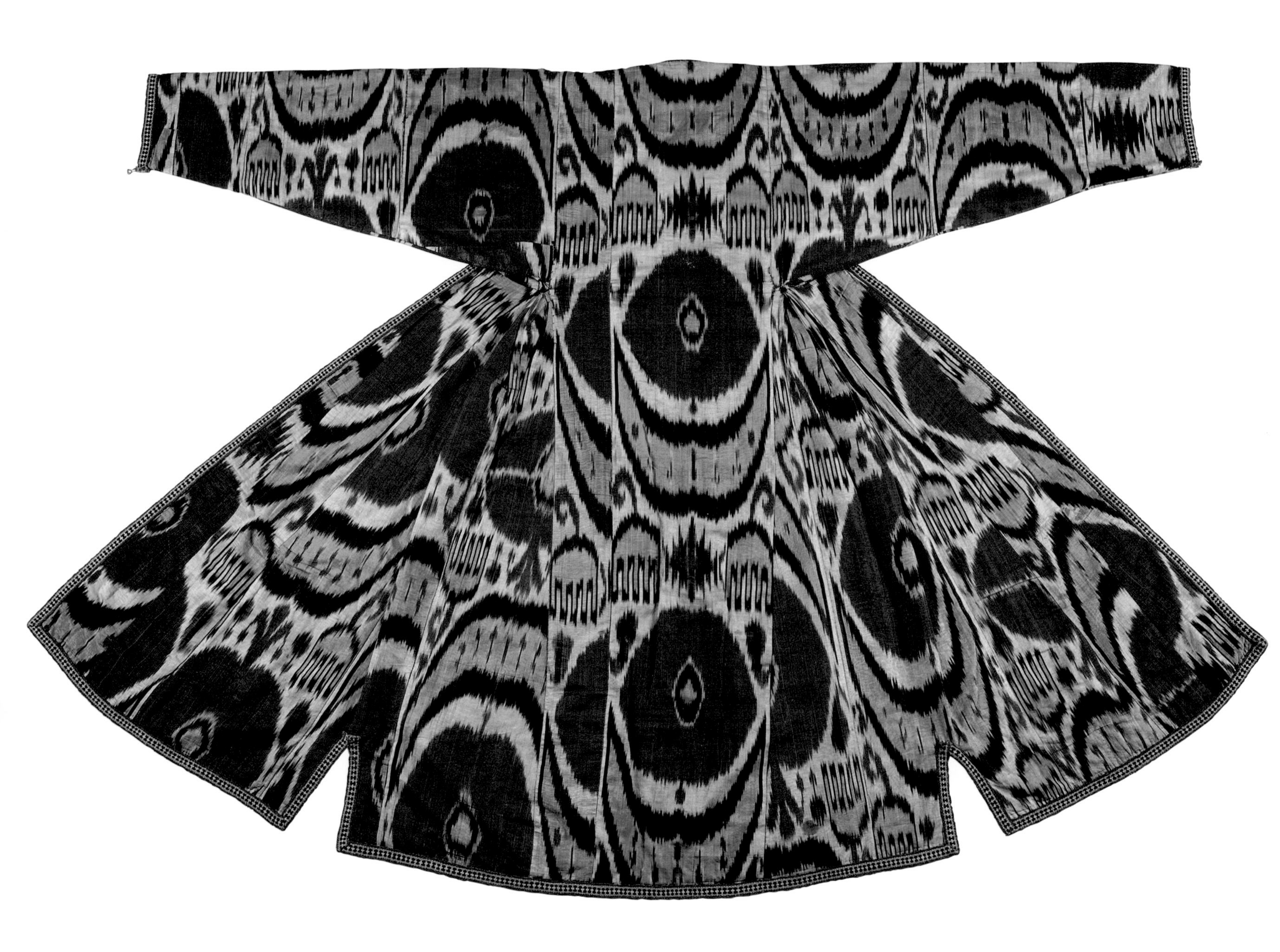

ABOVE Woman's robe. Silk and cotton, lined with printed cotton. 125.5 x 168cm
OPPOSITE Small wall hanging. Silk and cotton, backed with printed cotton. 60 x 40.8cm

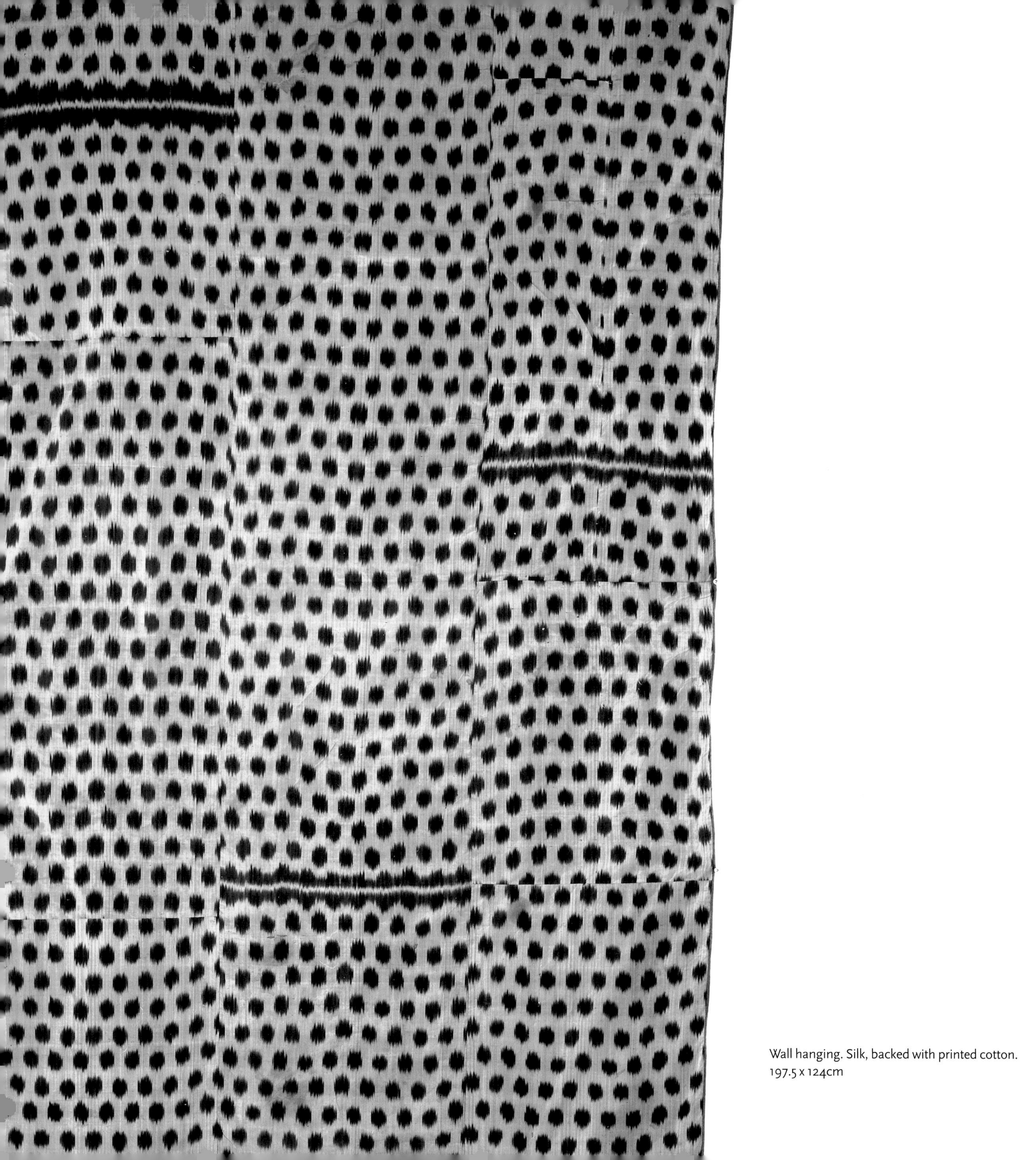

Wall hanging. Silk, backed with printed cotton.
197.5 x 124cm

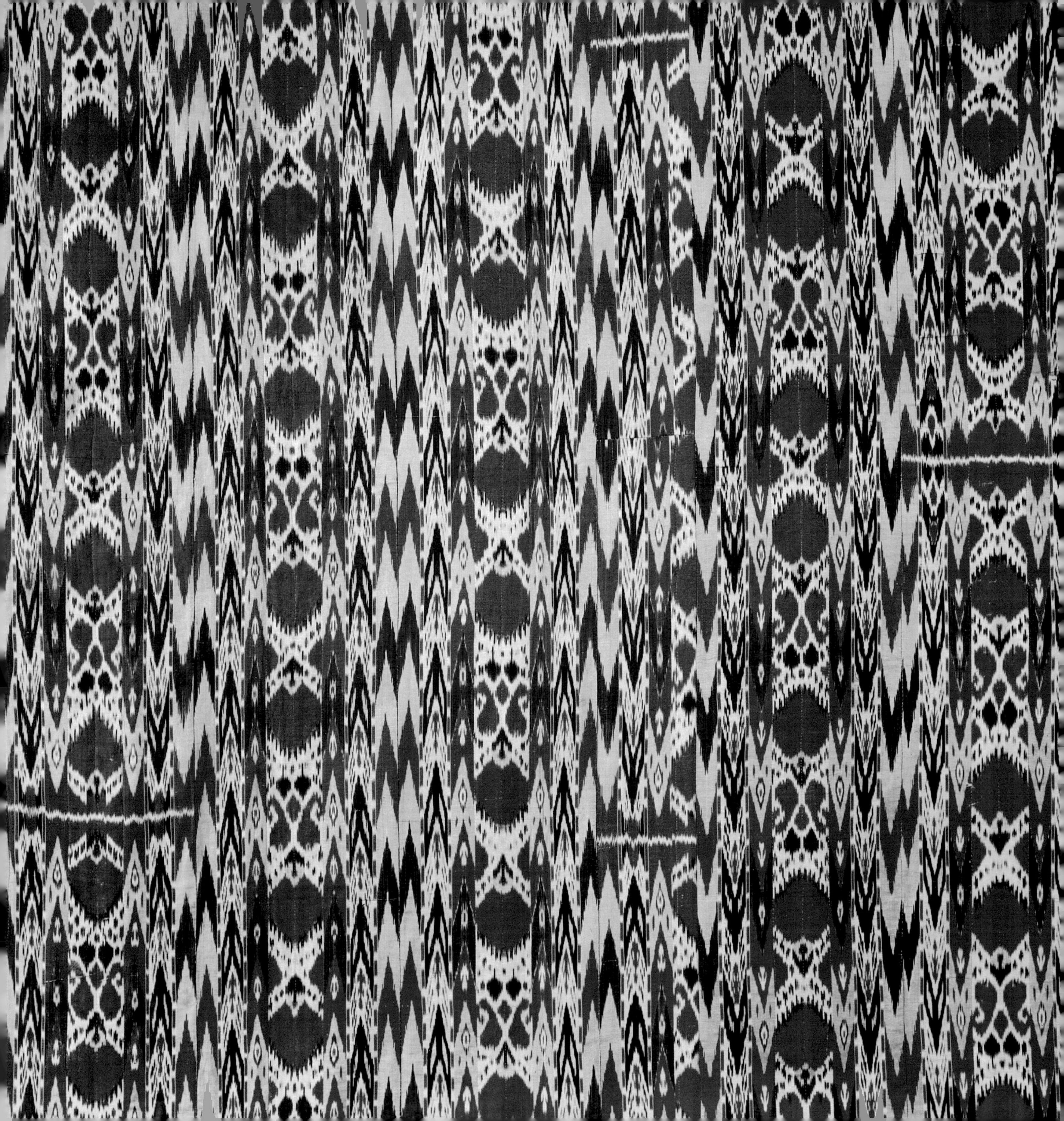

OPPOSITE Wall hanging (detail). Silk and cotton, backed with printed cotton. 217 x 158cm
ABOVE Woman's robe. Silk and cotton, lined with printed cotton. 126 x 132cm

OPPOSITE Wall hanging. Silk and cotton, backed with printed cotton. 202.5 x 132cm
RIGHT Wall hanging. Silk and cotton, backed with printed cotton. 129.5 x 97cm

Robe. Silk and cotton. After 1900. 127 x 168cm

Man's coat. Silk and cotton, lined with cotton.
After 1900. 148.5 x 209.5cm

ABOVE Man's robe. Silk and cotton, lined with printed cotton. After 1900. 145.5 x 220.5cm
OPPOSITE Man's robe. Silk and cotton, lined with printed cotton. After 1900. 118 x 165cm

Man's robe. Silk and cotton, lined with printed cotton. After 1900. 143 x 205cm

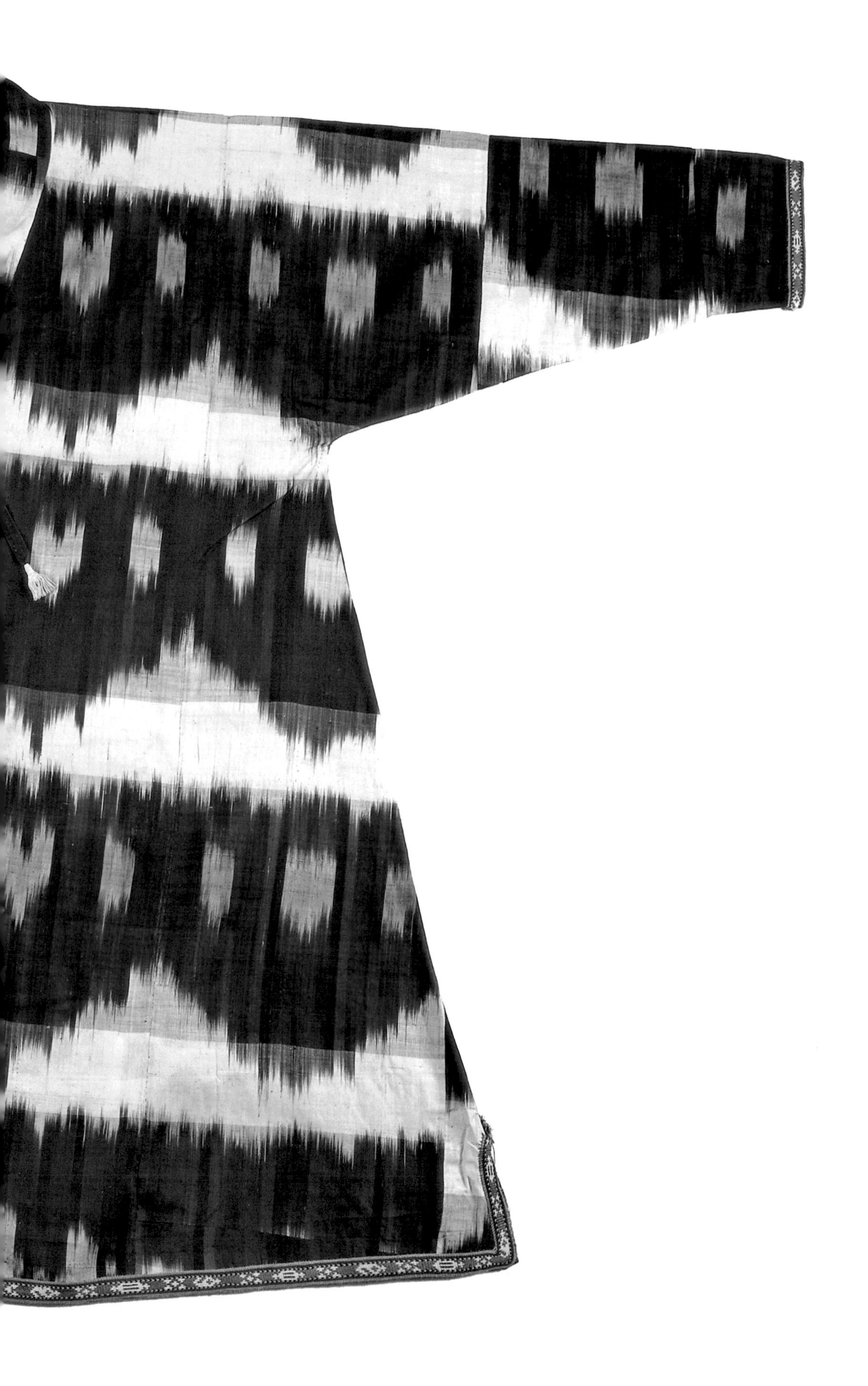

OPPOSITE Ikat length (detail). Silk and cotton with glaze. Before 1870. 30 x 540cm. V&A: 7941A(IS)
RIGHT Ikat length. Silk velvet. 67.8 x 128cm. V&A: T.30–1930

RIGHT Ikat length (detail). Silk and cotton. Before 1875. 40 x 125.6cm. V&A: 2112(IS)
OPPOSITE Ikat length (detail). Silk and cotton with glaze. Before 1875. 29 x 396.5cm. V&A: 2150A(IS)

Ikat length. Silk and cotton. 41.4 x 127.5cm.
V&A: IS 1366-1883

RIGHT Ikat length (detail). Silk and cotton. Before 1875. 41.8 x 178cm. V&A: 2110(IS)
OPPOSITE Ikat length (detail). Silk and cotton. Before 1875. 39.5 x 323cm. V&A: 2113(IS)

Ikat length. Silk and cotton with glaze.
Before 1875. 30.5 x 254cm. V&A: 2106(IS)

Notes

1 The relief is referred to and illustrated in Fitz Gibbon and Hale (1997), p.25
2 Fitz Gibbon and Hale (1997), pp.31–2
3 Shaw (1871)
4 Shaw (1871), pp.159–160
5 Shaw (1871), pp.173–4
6 Shaw (1871), p.174
7 Shaw (1871), p.263
8 Barnes (2005)
9 Fitz Gibbon and Hale (1997), p.221
10 Fitz Gibbon and Hale (1997), p.232
11 Rau (1988), p.14
12 See www.yordgorlik.uz

Bibliography

Barnes, R., 'Dressing for the Great Game: the Robert Shaw Collection in the Ashmolean Museum', *Khil'a* (2005), vol.1, pp.1–13
Fitz Gibbon, K. and Hale, A., *Ikat Silks of Central Asia* (London, 1997)
Guise, L. de (ed.), *Abrbandi – Ikats of Central Asia.* From the collection of the Islamic Arts Museum, Malaysia (Negara, 2006)
Harvey, J., *Traditional Textiles of Central Asia* (London, 1996)
Hasson, R., *Kaleidoscope of Colours – Silk Fabrics from Central Asia* (Jerusalem, 2004). From the Rau Collection, London
Kalter, J. and Pavaloi, M., *Uzbekistan – Heirs to the Silk Road* (London, 1997)
Rau, Pip, *Ikats – Woven Silks from Central Asia*, with an introduction by Andrew Hale and Kate Fitz Gibbon (Oxford, 1988)
Shaw, R., *Visits to the High Tartary, Yârkand and Kâshgar (formerly Chinese Tartary), and the Return Journey over the Karakoram Pass* (London, 1871)
Sumner, C., *Beyond the Silk Road – Arts of Central Asia* (2000)

Acknowledgements

The stunning ikat robes and hangings illustrated in this book are from the collection of Pip Rau. I extend my warmest thanks to her for allowing me access to these textiles for the purposes of this book, which accompanies the exhibition of Central Asian Ikats from the Rau collection at the V&A from November 2007 to March 2008. Her support for the project throughout and her openness in providing expertise and archival materials have been invaluable.

I would also like to take this opportunity to thank colleagues at the V&A who have supported my work on this project. I am particularly grateful to Rosemary Crill for her advice and support, and to all my colleagues in the Asian department for their patience and assistance. Thanks also to Pip Barnard for his work on the V&A photography.

Index

Page numbers in *italics* refer to illustrations.